Developing Mission Statements

Stefan Kühl is professor of sociology at the University of Bielefeld in Germany and works as a consultant for Metaplan, a consulting firm based in Princeton, Hamburg, Shanghai, Singapore, Versailles and Zurich. He studied sociology and history at the University of Bielefeld (Germany), Johns Hopkins University in Baltimore (USA), Université Paris-X-Nanterre (France) and the University of Oxford (UK).

Other Books by Stefan Kühl

Organizations: A Systems Approach
(Routledge 2013)
Ordinary Organizations: Why Normal Men Carried Out the Holocaust
(Polity Press 2016)
When the Monkeys Run the Zoo: The Pitfalls of Flat Hierarchies
(Organizational Dialogue Press 2017)
Sisyphus in Management: The Futile Search for the Optimal Organizational Structure
(Organizational Dialogue Press 2018)
The Rainmaker Effect: Contradictions of the Learning Organization
(Organizational Dialogue Press 2018)

To contact us:
Metaplan
101 Wall Street
Princeton, NJ 08540
USA
Phone: +1 609-688-9171
stefankuehl@metaplan.com
www.metaplan.com

Stefan Kühl

Developing Mission Statements

A Very Brief Introduction

Organizational Dialogue Press
Princeton, Hamburg, Shanghai, Singapore, Versailles, Zurich

ISBN (Print) 978-1-7323861-2-9
ISBN (EPUB) 978-1-7323861-3-6

Copyright © 2018 by Stefan Kühl

All rights reserved. No part of this publication may be reproduced or transmitted in any form or by any means, without permission in writing from the author.

Translated by: Lee Holt
Cover Design: Guido Klütsch
Typesetting: Thomas Auer
Project Management: Tabea Koepp
www.organizationaldialoguepress.com

Contents

Preface—Developing Models aside from
the Model of the Organization as Machine............................... 7

1.
What Are Mission Statements?—Introduction 12

   1.1 Mission Statements—Canons of Values in Organizations 16
   1.2 The Three Sides of Organization 17

2.
Beyond the Cascade Model of Organizations 35

   2.1 The Instrumental-Rational Model of Organization 35
   2.2 The Loose Connection between Visions, Missions, Strategies,
       Measures and Practices 37

3.
Developing Mission Statements outside of an Understanding of Organizations as Machines 40

   3.1 Between Harmonization and Identifying Contradictory Requirements 41

   3.2 Between Orientation towards Overarching Modes and the Specifics of an Organization 48

   3.3 Between Ideals and Describing the World 55

   3.4 The Same Mission Statement for Everyone, or Different Versions 57

   3.5 Mission Statements between Central Initiation and Decentral Anchoring 62

4.
The Relevance of the Mission Statement Process and Cultivating the Final Product—Conclusion 68

Bibliography 71

Preface—Developing Models aside from the Model of the Organization as Machine

Most manuals on creating and distributing mission statements are shaped by an understanding of the organization as something resembling a machine. Organizations are conceived upon the foundation of a purpose that then serves as a guideline for all organizational activity. There are attempts to define appropriate means for attaining these goals: the "optimal communication channels," the "right programs and agendas," and "suitable personnel." Under this notion of organizations, mission statements serve as orientation aids that all members are supposed to follow.

But unfortunately things aren't so simple. The reality of companies, administrations, armies, hospitals, universities, schools and associations looks much different than these machine-like images of organizations, because organizations are frequently not aware of their own purposes. Mission statements that are meant to provide points of orientation often regurgitate platitudes that could probably fit all of the organizations within an industry. Personnel in the various divisions and departments act as if they shared these guiding principles, but in actuality they pursue their own interests. The mission statement is proffered up on the stage, while cynical commentary runs backstage. Life in organizations seems to be much wilder than the dominant understanding of organizations as machines (which we find in self-help literature and in consulting documentation) would have us believe.

The aim of this brief volume in the *Management Compact* series is to show how the development of a mission statement—sometimes also referred to as a "credo," "guiding principles," "corporate philosophy" or "core values"—can go beyond the simplistic understanding of a mechanistic perception of organizations. We will show what function mission statements play as part of an organization's display side, how they relate to the formal structure, and how they interact with informal structures, or the organizational culture.

Our presentation of how mission statements develop relies on several years of experience in working on project management approaches with companies, ministries, administrations, universities, hospitals, and non-profit organizations. At specific points I show how our approach to the development of core values deviates from conventional practices and how we connect our findings to recent research on organizations.

Even if this book has emerged out of practical work on the creation of mission statements and is primarily oriented towards practitioners in organizations, I still believe that our approach resonates with insights from scholarly organizational theory. An approach informed by scholarship should not conceal the fact that the demands placed on scholarly texts are very different from those placed on texts for practitioners. While practical literature typically presents information in a tone of inspiration or pronouncements, scholarship is dominated by an evaluative, argument-driven tone. Practitioners like to repeat the words of the psychologist Kurt Lewin (Lewin 1951, 169), who said that nothing is more practical than a good theory. What they fail to understand, however, is the very different contexts of the origination of organizational practices and scientific findings about these practices. Even in the debate about the practical relevance of organizational studies (see for example the early discussion in Whitley 1984) and in research in applied sociology, people have repeatedly found that scholarly knowledge cannot be translated directly, without alteration, into practice.

In light of this unbridgeable difference between organizational science and organizational practice, I seek to introduce approaches to the creation and dissemination of mission statements that may have been inspired in one way or another by ideas from organizational theory, yet that are derived primarily from practical experience and have to prove themselves in the real world. There may be an idea here or there that is interesting to scholars; for example, when searching for the right way to attain a previously defined goal, there is a systematic differentiation between mission statements as formulations of values and strategies as programs for searching for resources. So, if a scholar finds some new material in this book, then all the better, but that is not my primary aspiration.

This small book is part of a series in which we present the essentials for the management of organizations against the backdrop of modern organizational theories. The *Management Compact* series includes this book as well as volumes on the subjects of *Developing Strategies, Designing Organizations, Influencing Organizational Culture, Managing Projects*, and *Exploring Markets*. In our book *Lateral Leading*, we assess how power, understanding and trust influence the management of organizations. Because we wrote these books at the same time, attentive readers will notice related trains of thought and similar formulations in all of the volumes in this series. These overlaps were created intentionally to emphasize the unity of the ideas behind the series and to highlight the connections between the volumes.

We do not believe in "simplifying" texts for managers and consultants by crowding our texts with bullet points, executive summaries, graphical presentations of how the text flows, or exercises. In most cases, such "supportive" methods infantilize readers by suggesting that they are not able to draw the central thoughts out of a book without help. That is why in this book, and in all of the other *Management Compact* volumes, we are very sparing with the use of visual aids. Along with a very limited number of graphics, there is only one element that makes reading easier. We use small boxes to introduce examples that give specific instances of our ideas, and we also use them to mark more extensive connections to organizational theory. Readers who are short on time or are not interested in these aspects can skip over the text boxes without losing the thread.

You can read more about the theoretical foundations of organizations in my book, *Organizations: A Very Brief Introduction*, which presents the limits of a machine model of organizations, oriented towards an ends-means schema, and an expansive understanding of organizations based on systems theory (Kühl 2011). Whoever is interested in mission statements in organizations can find more about this subject in *The Rainmaker Effect: Contradictions of the Learning Organization* and *Sisyphus in Management: The Futile Search for the Optimal Organizational Structure*.

This book was developed in the Metaplan training program, "Management and Consulting in Discourse." We would like to thank the participants for their input; they always critically assessed the approaches presented here and brought their practical experiences to the table. We are also grateful to those organizational scholars who have critiqued and commented upon Metaplan's practices in recent decades.

1. What Are Mission Statements?— Introduction

Whenever you download new software from mobile phone providers, the installation program will sometimes ask whether you would like to enter your personal "mission statement," your "individual credo." Most users may ask in irritation what consequences their mission statement may have in the future planning of their own work, or whether the phone will automatically reject all appointments that are not compatible with the mission statement. This makes it clear just how powerful the idea is that everyone today needs a mission statement.

According to estimates, 85% of all major U.S. companies had developed a mission statement by the turn of the millennium (Rigby 2003). The situation cannot be significantly different in Europe or Asia. Administrations, universities, hospitals, psychiatry clinics, armies, police forces, prisons, political parties and non-governmental organizations offer their employees, customers and suppliers a canon of values that seeks to offer guidance and orientation in the vague everyday life of organizations.

There are good reasons for the popularity of mission statements. In view of the difficulties inherent in exclusively hierarchical management of organizations, the catalogs of values—which, after all, are nothing other than mission statements—are associated with a hope that these principles can express, in a more abstract way, what kind of behavior organizations expect from their members.

And they should express what the receiver of services—customers of companies, patients in a hospital, or prisoners in a prison—can expect from the organization. In brief: mission statements should open up joint horizons of perception and thought.

Truly wondrous things are often expected from mission statements: one widespread notion is that mission statements help employees to identify with their organization's long-term goals. Mission statements are said to lead to increased commitment and improved performance, and to provide employees with orientation for their everyday actions and behaviors. Employees could become so independent that they can do "the right thing" to reach organizational goals. Decisions could be made faster and, above all, directly with the customer; more comprehensive coordination would be unnecessary. For the organization, core principles would lead to lower control costs, lower coordination costs, and to faster, more direct decision-making processes. This is supposed to lead to increased efficiency and growing flexibility (on such promises, see for example Bart 1997; Blair-Loy, Wharton, and Goodstein 2011).

As is the case for almost every other management trend, there are now studies on the phenomenon of the mission statement that try to verify its economic utility. In their book *Built to Last*, Jim Collins and Jerry I. Porras (Collins and Porras 2005) proclaim that, over a period of 50 years, the market value of companies with a corporate philosophy—such as Walmart, Boeing and 3M—was six times higher than companies without mission statements. In his book *The Committed Enterprise*, Hugh Davidson (Davidson 2002) promises that companies with a strong credo have customer satisfaction rates 16% above the market average and employee turnover 32% below average. Ira T. Kay and Bruce Pfau, in their book *Human Capital Edge* (Kay and Pfau 2001), claim that companies with a mission statement have a return on investment 29% higher than companies that do not have a mission statement or whose employees do not understand their corporate philosophy. Even if these figures are based on studies that are highly dubious in methodological terms, the message is quite clear: creating and working with mission statements pays off. The obverse case—namely, that the only organizations that craft mission statements are the ones that can afford it thanks to high profits—has not been researched.

So far, so good. Now that most companies, administrations, hospitals, schools and universities have their own mission statements, many have already overhauled them two or three times, and some departments in companies, administrations or faculties at universities have developed canons of values for their respective units, mission statements are increasingly coming under critique. These critical voices really crank up the volume when economically difficult times come around, clamoring for putting aside the work on mission statements so that they can concentrate on the really important aspects of the business.

It has become very clear that cynicism poses the greatest risk factor in the creation and propagation of mission statements. Top management often does not notice that employees, as well as customers and suppliers, sometimes react with irony, scorn or cynicism when confronted with a corporate philosophy. And the tenser the economic situation is, the more exacerbated the discrepancy between the noble phrases of the mission statement and the everyday reality of organizations.

Here are just a few examples. The employees at an automobile manufacturer comment with delicious irony on their orders from above to always have the company's new mission statement, printed on a plastic card, in their work suit. Members of the German Navy recently received a canon of values, so sailors recite the mission statement as dictated to them by the military leadership in seminars, although with an ironic undertone. Or we look at a division of a major electronics company that dismisses several workers while simultaneously holding up a values statement about trust that also manages to alienate the workers who remain.

The mass media also comment on mission statements with increasingly gleeful sarcasm. One commentator has noted that hardly a single mission statement has been spared from this debate. There is an endless list of companies and institutions that have decided to draft a mission statement. It is becoming increasingly difficult, one commentator has noted, to escape all of these "little administrative visions," all of them "a bit simple-minded," let alone to bear the imposition of their "cognitive sub-complexity."

The process of creating a mission statement seems to be a very sensitive matter for a company, administration or hospital. And *not* because a mission statement can have devastating effects on an organization's practices. A mission statement is far too abstract for an organization to fall apart because of anything derived from the mission statement. What is instead becoming increasingly clear is how high the risk for an organization is whenever it declares its values through mission statements. The values and moral ideas that people claim as their own always awaken suspicion among their target audience that such statements may just be assurances that are quickly forgotten when the going gets rough.

1.1 Mission Statements— Canons of Values in Organizations

If someone in an administration, a company, school or political party asks about a mission statement, someone reaches into a drawer and pulls out a multi-page document, typically printed on high-gloss paper. This document proclaims positive-sounding principles that organizational members should feel bound to, and they are expected to comply with them.

But beyond this immediate association with a couple of pages of nice-sounding statements, it really remains unclear what exactly a mission statement is supposed to be. The idea of the mission statement is so dazzling that it can take on all kinds of different meanings: the values shared by all of the organization's members, the guidelines for actions in the organization, the image that the organization is supposed to present to the outside world, the organizational culture or norms that the organization aspires to and to which the members should orient themselves.

In the language of systems theory, mission statements are nothing more than a *canon of values* that is proclaimed inwardly and outwardly. When we think of values, we think of the following kinds of statements: "We protect our environment," "We are handicapped accessible," "Our employees are our most important resource," or "The customer is king." These may present broad behavioral expectations, yet they leave open the question of what actions can be expected in a specific situation. Due to their abstractness, values may have "high chances at consensus" (Luhmann 1972, 88f.), yet they are also packed full of practical contradictions. How far should you go to protect "our environment"? Are you allowed in an emergency to kill for it? How should you behave if something serves the "king customer," yet harms the employees, the company's "most important resource"?

Values are abstract and lead to contradictions at the same time, and they are fundamentally different from *programs*. Programs are rules for proper decision-making. They can come along in the form of strategies—for example in an agreement to win over 15% more customers by the end of the year, or to raise revenues by 10%. The highlight of programs, however, is that—unlike values—you can identify, in a comparatively certain way, whether actions have followed or deviated from the program. It is easy to determine whether 15% more customers have been won over within a year, or if revenue has been increased by 10%. But figuring out whether a customer has been treated like a king is open to a variety of interpretations.

1.2 The Three Sides of Organization

To better understand what a mission statement is and what functions it plays in an organization, we must first differentiate between the three sides of an organization (see the extensive discussion in Kühl 2011, 89ff.). The *display side* is the facade of an organization. It is meant to present something by means of its embellishments, ornamentation, or perhaps its evenness (Rottenburg 1996, 191ff.). Organizations present the most attractive facade possible to the outside world so that they can attract customer favor, influence the media to attain the best possible coverage, or to receive legitimation through political forces. What happens in the back of the "business" is not completely unimportant, but survival in an organization depends in many cases significantly on whether the "facade" is properly decorated with "display windows." If we take a look at the mission statements published by companies, administrations, hospitals, schools and prisons, it is clear that they play an important function for the organization's display side. The *formal side* is about the official body of rules to which members feel bound. Mission statements implicitly claim that the principles propagated on the display side are directly reflected in the organization's formal structure. The mission statement principles presented on the display side, it is suggested, are also the principles that guide the actions of the organization's members as a formal structure. The *informal side* of an organization, on the other hand, consists of long-established practices and ways of thinking, of regular deviations from official rules, from cultivated myths, dogmas and fictions. The (overly) ambitious claim of mission statement processes is often that the principles broadcast inwardly and outwardly correlate strongly to the organization principles that dominate the informal side of the organization.

How do canons of values from mission statements affect these three sides of organizations?

The Celebration of Values—Mission Statements as Part of an Organization's Display Side

Because mission statements consist of articulations of values, the abstractness of which meets with broad consensus, they are ideally suited for an organization's display side. This is because

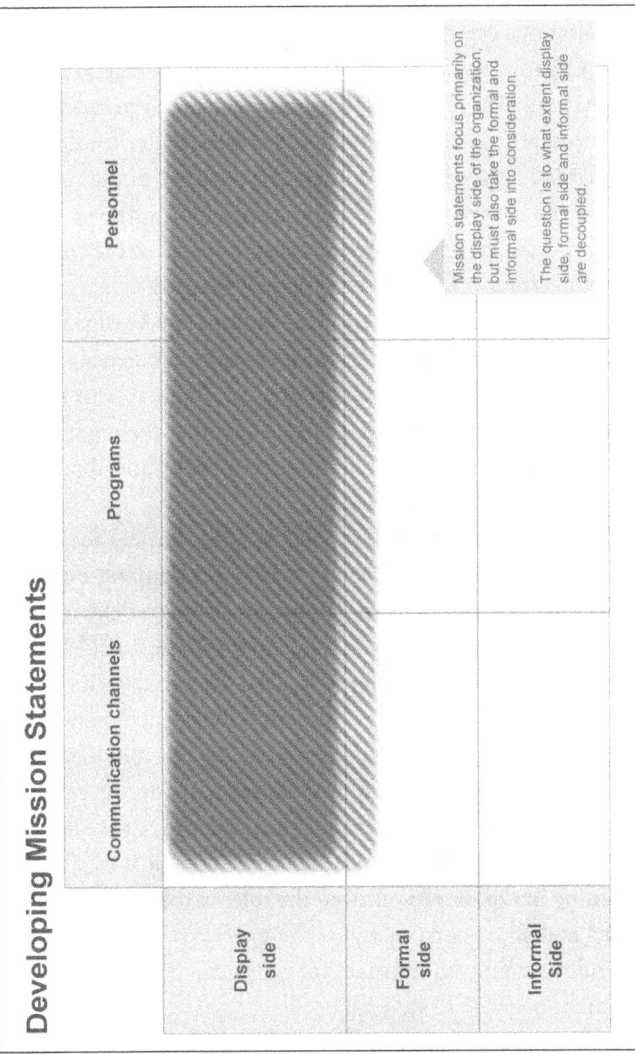

Diagram 1: The structure matrix for analyzing organizations—mission statements between the display side and the informal side.

organizations express on their display side how they want to be seen. Organizations typically try on their display side to paint as consistent a picture as possible. Terms such as "corporate design" or "corporate communication" are manifestations of attempts to standardize symbolism within an organization so that external parties can always recognize the organization. In the ideal case, the corporate designers create a uniform image of the company by such varied means as coffee cups, the gardens around the building, and the hand towels in the bathrooms. An organization can however follow a strategy of presenting differences against the backdrop of a uniform appearance. References to various styles of clothing and language can signal that the organization is comprised of very different types of people, and that this is precisely what makes it special.

Display sides have an important task, namely to protect the inside of the organization. It is about denying outsiders insight into the company so that decisions can be deliberated in peace, or concealing possible conflicts from the outside world, or hiding mistakes or embarrassments. We can describe this as a "concealment" or "disguise" function that facades play. Organizations typically follow their procedures for manufacturing a product, preparing an administrative decision, or planning course offerings at a university, in a way that conceals these preparations from outsiders. This is not done just for the sake of hiding minor deviations from the rules in the form of artifice, tricks and short-cuts; many of the processes that conform to the rules are only appropriate for outsiders to a limited degree (Luhmann 1964, 114).

Decoupling from the Formal Structure—Mission Statements and Their Relationship to the Formal Structure

The major weakness of canons of value is that they are not suited to the formulation of specific formal expectations of organization members. Formal expectations are those expectations that an organizational member must fulfill to continue being a member of the organization. The formal expectations specify from what time to what time a person has to be present in the organization. They determine what someone has to do while they are there, which other organization members deserve attention and who can be ignored. If someone is not ready to align themselves with these formal expectations, then they cannot remain a member of the organization.

In order to be able to make a specific behavior a prerequisite for membership, the organization's demands on its members must be specific and consistent. It is relatively difficult to accuse a colleague of misconduct if the organization calls for her to comply with such abstract values as collegiality and motivation to perform, which are behaviors that in specific situations can be mutually exclusive. It is difficult to reproach a manager if such abstract, potentially contradictory demands are made on her, for example, to elevate customer expectations to the foremost consideration in her actions while simultaneously viewing employees as the organization's most important resources.

Of course there are inconsistent expectations in every organization. Every member of an organization can tell you a thing or two about that. But it is precisely the contradictions of the formal body of rules that allow members to elude behavioral expectations; in these spaces of ambiguity, they can refer to the rule that they prefer to follow. The reaction to too many contradictions is often to try to clean things up and establish order. Attempts by organizations to flag behaviors as formal membership requirements lead to consistent observance and compliance with the rules. The canons of values created for the display side, however, can include the parallel articulation of various expectations that turn out to be contradictory in the everyday life of the organization. This happens because these canons of values are typically not written down in a specific way.

By looking at the difference between strategies and mission statements, we can clarify the difference between measures that aim more at the formal side of organizations and measures that aim at the display side, with their externally oriented canons of values. When we talk about strategies, we mean acting in a way that works toward the attainment of specified targets, in situations where those responsible have to reckon with sanctions if they do not attain the formalized goals. Mission statements, on the other hand, are, like all other articulations of values, substantially more abstract than strategic objectives. Although the values transported by mission statements deliver preferences for actions, they still leave open which action should be favored over another. They merely provide a general frame for orientation and, unlike strategic objectives, cannot serve as an aid for specific decision-making problems. To put it differently, mission statements are "non-instructive strategies."

EXAMPLE

Example: Various Groups in a Company Interpret a Mission Statement

A project within an automobile manufacturer's major engine factory decides to incorporate the principle of "self-regulation" into their mission statement. The project managers have decided to use the idea of "self-regulation"—meaning the exercise of one's own responsible control over work that creates value—because they would like to avoid the term "group work," which has a somewhat negative charge in the company and is the subject of political struggles.

At first glance, you might think that it is clear to all of the participants what this means: to combine all of the planning, organizing and controlling functions in the assembly division with its operative functions and to put them in one person's hands.

What we see, however, is that the mission statement is used in very different ways (some of them contradictory) by the various groups of actors. The management uses it to legitimate the dismantling of activities that do not create immediate value; the works council uses it to call for the dismantling of hierarchies; department heads point to the mission statement to justify the outsourcing of tasks and the accumulation of responsibility.

The idiosyncratic feature of mission statements is that they are so abstract that they are a poor foundation for specific recommendations of action. Mission statements typically do not provide concrete guidance in a conflict situation as to whether a decision should be made for the benefit of the customer, the shareholder, the supplier, or the company. The mission statement does not determine whether the employee—as required in the corporate philosophy—decides to take the risk of making a good-faith mistake while pursuing innovation, or, when the rubber meets the road, decides to take a safer yet less innovative path to deliver a reliable product.

In practice, it is not easy to differentiate between the development of mission statements and the formulation of strategic goals, because the formulations of values in the mission statements always point the way to a certain kind of action. A commitment to the guiding principle of decentralization of decision-making processes would only come across as somewhat convincing, if it were not offered as a catalog of criteria for specific decision-making situations. A commitment to the value of employee orientation would lose its persuasive power if, at the same time, a message is not sent so that people know that this orientation is not meant to induce immediate action, and that it must defer to the orientation towards efficiency if conflict arises.

THEORY

How Can We Tell Whether an Organization's Values Are Formulated as a Strategy or as a Mission Statement?

Articulations of strategies and mission statements are often very similar in their descriptions. This is why it is important to be able to identify, during the process, what exactly you are working on—strategies or core values. When shaping processes related to a corporate philosophy or mission statement, we use four tests to enable the marking of differences between the development of a strategy and of a mission statement.

1. The Agreement Test

We ask the following questions in our agreement tests: Can someone within the organization take up an explicit position against this value? What would happen if the chairman of the board or the managing director spoke out directly against this value?

Example: Infineon, in its mission statement, listed values such as "Our customer's success is the goal of our actions," "Drive and energy define our actions," "We actively shape our future and thereby take on challenges and risks with confidence," and "Results and maximum achievements are the driving force of our actions and decision-making." To make clear that they are talking about mission statements and not about strategies, you could point out for example that "Drive and energy define the actions of Infineon" and then ask who is against this statement. If everyone can agree on this statement, then it is very likely that we are dealing with a value.

2. The Tautology Test

When justifying the values in mission statements, there is a strong tendency to engage in tautologies. Tautologies are self-referential constructions. The statement, "This sentence is correct," cannot be rebutted because of its tautological construction. The sentence is both a statement and the subject of the statement; it confirms itself. In its simplest form, a tautology says something like, "A diesel motor is a diesel motor is a diesel motor" and everyone can see it for what it is. It is slightly more difficult to identify tautologies when they conceal a semantic equation by using different terms: "Create innovative product development."

Aloys Gälweiler has proposed a simple test for checking whether a concept is a tautology. Gälweiler notes that a statement is tautological if, when you negate the recommendation, this results in an unworkable alternative. If, for example, the management guru Stephen R. Covey recommends that you react proactively to surprises, you can recognize the tautological character of this admonition if you negate it. We cannot assume that surprises will not surprise us. Covey is also right when he proposes that we complete our most important tasks first; ultimately, however, we find the recommendation to complete the most important tasks just before the deadline as a less helpful alternative.

Example: If we take a look at the mission statement of the innovative company 3M, we see examples of the company's shared values, such as "absolute integrity," "respect for individual initiative," tolerance for errors "made in good faith," and "high-quality and reliable products." To negate these statements, we could say that "merely partial integrity" is important, that "there is no need to respect individual initiative," that "errors are excepted, even if they are made in bad faith," and that people are prepared to offer "customers low-quality and unreliable products."

3. The Evaluation Test

When it comes to the values espoused in mission statements, the question comes up, just like for strategies, as to whether people act in accordance with the value in question. If a political party focuses on the environment, women's rights, fighting poverty or human rights, then they have to ask themselves whether their own actions contribute to the attainment of these values. But mission statements pose the difficulty that it is never possible to say with completely certainty whether a value has been attained or not.

For strategies, on the other hand, it is relatively easy to see the attainment or non-attainment of an ideal, because strategies have a high degree of certainty. For example, calculations would show whether a target of earning 10% of revenues from a new market segment was reached or not. There are ways to identify with relative clarity whether a goal of moving 20% of workers from a center in Paris to countries outside of Europe has been reached or not.

Example: Nokia describes its mission as "Connecting People": "By connecting people, we help fulfill a fundamental human need for social connections and contact. Nokia builds bridges between people—both when they are apart and face-to-face—and also bridges the gap between people and the information they need." It is impossible to evaluate whether or not Nokia has reached these goals. How can we know whether bridges have been built between people? How should we measure whether Nokia has granted "people" access to the information they need?

4. The Value Hierarchization Test

Another criterion for recognizing values in mission statements is that values typically evade clear hierarchization, and in the event that they allow themselves to be arranged into a hierarchy, they lose their character as values. In contrast, strategies arrange such aspects in a hierarchical way. The decision to enter the mid-range car segment necessarily means—when resources are limited—that the company has to abandon the development of other market segments.

The test question asks whether the various values can be arranged in a hierarchical manner. Is an orientation towards shareholders more important than an orientation towards employees? When conflicts arise, do people always make decisions that benefit the customer and not the employee? Mission statements often dispense with the hierarchization of values and promote instead their compatibility. Social aid organizations have mission statements that promote values such as human rights, environmental protection, economic dynamism, help for those who need it most, and the proper use of tax revenues. All of these are values that are assumed, in an abstract way, to not just be compatible with one another, but also to somehow mutually support and reinforce each other. People simply block out the fact that these various values frequently lead to conflicts in specific decision-making situations in development work.

Example: IBM put forward a mission statement for a long time that proclaimed "customer service," "obligations to shareholders," "fair treatment of suppliers," and "social responsibility." But was top management ready to prioritize these values? Would a top manager at IBM be ready to say that "customer service" is more important than "obligations to shareholders?" Or would IBM be ready to say that, in an emergency, increasing profits for shareholders should be done at the cost of "social responsibility"? Probably not.

Mission Statements and Informal Structures— The Tense Relationship with Organizational Culture

Management places a lot of hope in the idea that a mission statement can influence an organization's culture—the informal structures—of a company, an administration, a hospital, or a school. The process for articulating a mission statement revives an old management dream: the hope that the process can shape informal networks, hidden incentive structures, and implicit ways of thinking in such a way that they work in the context of the company. A mission statement, as a malleable success factor, is supposed to get a handle on the "soft factors" in an organizational culture. According to this thesis, the success of a company, administration or university does not depend primarily on its formal organizational structure, but rather on the culture, and this is thought to be subject to influence via corporate philosophy.

The challenge, however, is that the organizational culture—which is located in the informal structures—evades the direct grasp of management. We call expectations in an organization "informal" when they *cannot* be articulated in relation to the membership conditions. A manager can bring informal expectations to her employees—for example, to work longer hours than is stipulated by law—yet, if they do not meet this expectation, she cannot issue a written warning saying that her informal expectations of her direct reports have not been fulfilled. The legal department of an administration, the military court of an army, and the arbitration board of a political party would lose a trial if they had to admit that one of their employees may have violated an organization's informal expectations, yet acted properly in formal terms.

Informality is often willfully misunderstood as the "refuge of humanity," the human relationships in the "hard steel housing" of organizations. This is where people can still be people, while elsewhere the hard ideas communicated through the organization about "exploitative conditions of capitalism," "ideologies of bureaucratic administration," or "alienated labor" are thought to be operative. Many still believe that the informal side offers a space in which an emotional, playful interaction among people can develop, while elsewhere they are expected to function like cogs in a machine.

This attempt to describe informality with humanizing prose is misleading though. The rites of initiation that boarding schools, army units or fraternities put their initiates through before joining the organization, some of which are informal, are not always compatible with the UN Charter for Human Rights. The methods that cliques use in organizations to enforce their informal expectations are frequently more brutal then the intervention tools held by the boss, which are limited by their formality.

EXAMPLE

"Demigods of the Docks"—Organizational Culture at a Container Terminal

Day laborers were recruited as dockworkers in the nineteenth century. They would gather in the morning on the quay wall and wait to be chosen for loading and unloading ships; they would then pick up their pay packet in dockside pubs selected for that purpose. Those who selected the workers were powerful people who wielded the power to make decisions about wages and bread, about who received coveted extra work, who was allowed to work during the day or night, or even who was assigned to the dirtiest jobs.

As time went by, increasing numbers of workers found permanent jobs and working conditions in port operations, which were subject to co-determination regulations, improved noticeably. Today, permanent employees are no longer required to work all of the weekend or night shifts. In periods of peak demand, there are always labor shortages if all employees have already fulfilled their shift quotas.

But those doing the choosing still decide over who is assigned to which ship. According to one port worker, they are the "demigods of the docks—that's just the port culture." These "demigods" continue to make decisions about money and amenities. Are you assigned to a ship where there's going to be a lot of overtime, or to a ship where the work may run out before the shift is even over? Do you get a vehicle with or without a radio? Are you working with a colleague that you can rely on? Do you get the shifts you want, or are you suddenly and spontaneously assigned to tomorrow's night shift?

On one hand, when there are peak periods of work, these coordinators have to think about finding workers who will work overtime spontaneously and voluntarily. On the other hand, they can make the shifts pleasant or unpleasant for workers and distribute well-paid overtime hours. This means that there is a lively bartering scene between coordinators and dockworkers, and this takes place outside of the collective wage agreements.

Because the assignment of overtime, devices or shifts is done on the basis of formal decisions, "deal making" may not be compatible with the formal structure, but it is a tolerated informal act. The power of these coordinators is not God-given or rooted in the harbor's history; the daily struggle plays a functional role for the organization: the coordinators are in a position to plan staff allocation relatively quickly because, with these small deals, they can make formal demands for overtime that are binding. There is cooperation and wheeling and dealing, but in a completely different way than the inventors of the port's core values imagined.

It becomes clear why an organizational culture influenced by a mission statement does not serve, contrary to the occasional hopes of management, as a magic bullet that solves management problems in companies, administrations or hospitals. The idea of organizational culture has become a kind of fetish that does two things: first, it serves as a superficial renunciation of classical notions of management and control; and second, it covertly enables the maintenance of order, even if it is more difficult to access. The opportunities to exercise direct influence on an organization's culture, however, are limited.

The problem is that management may be able to work on an ideal image of its organizational culture, to spend lots of money on developing mission statements by and for their employees, and to engage in real effusions of humanistic prose in workshops, but in the end, there is no certainty that this cultural program will end up sticking with employees. Well-rehearsed patterns of thought, values and attitudes, and informal standards of action in organizations cannot be controlled in a rational way, programmed in formal terms, and administered with technocratic means; that is the character of informal structures. An organization's culture emerges "on its own." This does not exclude transformation, but "transformation cannot be introduced as change, nor by decree" (Luhmann 2000, 243, 245).

Worse still, if management commits in its soapbox speeches or glossy mission statements to a set of cultural values, it always arouses the suspicions in their target audience that they are just paying lip service to these ideals. There is a certain similarity between organizational culture and sex: if you're talking about it too much, you probably don't have it. The foundation of the organization therefore reacts to organizational cultural programming from above with cynicism.

Given the limited efficacy of officially proclaimed canons of values, organizations have to ask themselves the following questions: What functions can a mission statement fulfill? And how can the process of formulating a mission statement prevent cynicism as an unwanted side effect of the mission statement? How can you create a mission statement process outside of the context of instrumental-rational ideas about management and control?

2. Beyond the Cascade Model of Organizations

Classical paradigms of mission statement development, which are shaped by an understanding of organizations as machines, viewed the mission statement for years as the starting point for all decisions that followed. The way to start, the long-proposed approach says, is to articulate a vision as a fundamental idea of the organization's future role. This vision is then supposed to be specified in a mission statement, which also provides information about the organization's values. The mission statement then forms the basis for a cascade-like process of formulating strategic goals. The cascade is supposed to end with a list of measures for implementing the strategy, and the tenets of the corporate philosophy are supposed to soak into the organization's culture. The idea is that every step in the process lays down an additional layer of foundation, working downwards as if towards the base of a pyramid.

2.1 The Instrumental-Rational Model of Organization

This cascade-shaped thinking is mirrored in a variety of recent management concepts. In the Balanced Scorecard model, the measurement figures are derived from the vision and mission of the company, administration or hospital (Kaplan and Norton

1996). In the Closed Loop Management System for strategy development, every strategic consideration begins with the preparation of a "vision statement," a "mission statement," and a "value statement" (Kaplan and Norton 2008). Quality models such as the EFQM model assume that a clear mission statement is the point of departure for the implementation of quality requirements.

The entire organization is derived from an uppermost purpose. The head of the organization defines a general goal to be pursued (for example, "We want to be the leading pharmaceutical company in the field of oncology"). Then resources and methods are selected with which this overarching goal can be best attained ("We want to bring to market at least four blockbuster pharmaceuticals with more than one billion in revenue"). The defined means for attaining this goal are then translated into subgoals, and means for attaining these goals are identified ("We will buy a company that has this kind of blockbuster medication"). This creates a hierarchical chain of upper and lower goals that enable the structuring of every act in the organization (March and Simon 1958, 191).

At first glance, this approach has quite a bit of charm because it suggests a high degree of organizational stringency. Management may fantasize that the various processes in the organization interlock together as in a machine. The result is a streamlined organization in which all of the constituent elements consistently relate to one another. This model satisfies the hopes of top managers who believe in the illusion presented by the cascade model, which suggests that, in principle, all decisions in an organization can be derived from fundamental ideas.

2.2 The Loose Connection between Visions, Missions, Strategies, Measures and Practices

Reality in organizations, however, looks completely different. It is more often the case that organizations first decide on strategic directions, and then plan for them. Then the mission statements and visions come afterwards, to give the whole project the impression of a consistent logic. Often, innovative employees initiate practices that then create previously non-existent opportunities for new strategies. Visions then develop on the basis of these practices, which are introduced from the lower levels of the organization. Sometimes, strategies and mission statements are driven forward independently of one another and developed by completely different people in the organization. In such cases, they are then—to use the language of recent organizational research—only loosely connected (Weick 1976).

The causal relationships between visions, missions, strategies, measures and practices are only bent into shape with laborious verbal acrobatics in order to convey the appearance of coherence. A measure is presented as though it resulted almost inevitably from a specific strategy. An approved strategy is trimmed in such a way that it creates the impression that the strategy was derived from a vision. Sometimes this reminds us of the good old days of state socialism, in which every restructuring of a collective or every purchase of a machine by an agricultural production collective was presented as the means to meet the targets of a statewide five-year plan, or even as a direct quote from the collected works of Marx and Engels.

Deviations from the "true teachings," according to the logic of the instrumental-rational model of organizations, only lead to an even stronger propagation of the cascade model. In this context, if everyday practice deviates from the ideas in the plan, then this is bad for everyday practice; people don't see this, though, as an occasion to rethink the principles of management concepts. For management pioneers, organizational consultants and change specialists, this leads to a field of activity that is in principle unlimited, because they can present practitioners in organizations with ever new, revised models for ever more elaborate, cascade-shaped organizational planning.

In our experience, it does not make sense in the mission statement process to juxtapose the reality of organizations again and again with a pure cascade model. Instead, we should refer to the phenomenon of the loose connection between the development of mission statements and strategies. Work on mission statements, visions and values takes place at an abstract level, largely emancipated from the bitter realities of the organization. The strategic development process, in contrast, is only loosely coupled and pointed towards central decisions in the organization.

This decoupling is important because the development of mission statements on one hand and strategies on the other fulfill very different, sometimes opposing functions. According to the Swedish organizational researcher Nils Brunsson (Brunsson 1989), organizations have to produce fundamental "decisions" in the form of strategies while also generating "talk," for example in the form of mission statements. This "sugarcoated speech," says Brunsson, is necessary so that organizations can satisfy the diverse demands of their employees, cooperation partners, customers, and the mass media, without this kind of talk having an immediate and direct effect on actual decision-making processes.

A manager who is striving for "authenticity" will find it difficult to accept the fact that he has to produce both fundamental decisions (in the form of strategies) and "talk" (in the form of mission statements). Yet organizations have no other way to meet the growing number of opposing demands. If they were to try to bring order to these contradictory claims, they would begin to despair. Mission statements therefore offer the possibility of being consistent at the level of "talk" and then making decisions in practice as they are needed.

3. Developing Mission Statements outside of an Understanding of Organizations as Machines

When preparing mission statements, "catch-all" statements always have spontaneous plausibility; "We do everything that belongs to modern human resources work" sounds good at first. Working on people *and* on organizational structures; consulting on experts *and* processes; peace *and* freedom—or as was often said in the 1970s, "peace, love and happiness." These ideas sound good because they suggest that everything can be optimized at the same time; we optimize people, and we optimize the organizational structure. We are experts in a particular issue and simultaneously shape the processes. We are getting peace, freedom, joy, and we get to eat our cake too.

In the realm of abstract thought, people can always believe in these kinds of both/and constructions: they really shine as statements in political speeches, on campaign posters, and the mission statements of companies and administrations. In his consideration of the Christian Democratic Union party of Germany (CDU), sociologist Niklas Luhmann (Luhmann 1977) points out that contradictions in all organizations are quickly "homogenized at the level of language." On the subject of education, the Christian Democrats called simultaneously for equal opportunity and the division of young students into different schools designed for blue collar, white collar and academic professions—as if these two goals could be realized in parallel. In terms of the political system, Luhmann noted that CDU politicians called for observance of laws on one hand and moral responsibility on the other, without noting that conflicts could arise between these values and that this kind of canon of values was also similar to that of other political parties.

With these kinds of willy-nilly collections of "great values," organizations suggest that they hold their employees, clients or voters to be rather naive. The contradictions between these values that are propagated in parallel are often so glaring that anyone can clearly see that some of the proclaimed values can exist only at the cost of another value.

In the following, we will discuss five principles that will show how a mission statement process can go beyond simple catch-all phrases, and what effects this can have, despite all of the limits of this instrument.

3.1 Between Harmonization and Identifying Contradictory Requirements

Every company and every hospital, every university, and—to take an example that is probably exotic for people in the corporate world—every police organization has to put up with contradictions in values. Companies have to fulfill the expectations of their customers, shareholders and employees—requirements that are not always compatible. Hospitals for example have to ensure the best possible medical care for their patients, support research on illnesses, and make sure that enough money is coming into their coffers. Universities move between such different demands as excellence in research and concentration on teaching—conditions that are probably only possible in a professor's wildest dreams. On one hand, the police have to catch as many criminals as possible, yet they have to comply with legal regulations that frequently limit their ability to do so.

Organizations could now try to bring these different, often competing values into a clear ranking, and thereby offer clear orientation to their employees. A company can commit to the idea that profit is its only maxim and ignore all other values. Or a university could attempt, when making decisions about resources, to focus principally on providing outstanding teaching and accept that research activities will take a back seat.

The establishment of such clear rankings however always means a loss of possible actions. If a company sets up a focus on profit in such a resolute way that employee satisfaction or regional acceptance becomes irrelevant, it will quickly run into difficulties with legitimacy. A company that announces that its only goal is "profit, profit, profit," will run into problems explaining itself. Employees want to have the feeling that the eight, nine or ten hours they spend working every day aren't just for filthy lucre; they want to feel that they are part of something greater. Customers can develop more loyalty to a company if they believe that they really are the focal point of the company's interest, not that they are being milked like dairy cows. A university that concentrates on excellence in the education of managers and physicians can run into major problems if research achievements are not up to snuff.

Ultimately organizations never manage to completely resolve their internal contradictions because the expectations placed on organizations are already contradictory. But the question of organizational integration comes up again and again. Articulations of values in the form of mission statements or corporate philosophies are, in the final analysis, a reaction to these contradictory values. "Give me a mission statement"—shortly after German reunification, this was the ironic motto of the Volksbühne theater in former East Berlin. This was a pointed comment made by East Germans after the fall of the Berlin Wall about the new cocktail of values swirling around them, a mixture of parliamentary democracy and a market economy.

In the classical paradigm of mission statement creation, companies, administrations, hospitals and universities have insisted on concealing or covering up the contradictions that confront organizations and their employees. One of IBM's first mission statements proclaimed a simultaneous commitment to "customer service," "obligations to shareholders," "fair treatment of suppliers," and "social responsibility." This suggested that the interests of employees, suppliers, shareholders, customers and social interest groups did not conflict, and that IBM and its employees could be satisfied in parallel. One of the first versions of the mission statement for McDonald's promised that McDonald's could be "many things at the same time": "employer," "social partner," "franchise partner," "quality manager," and "much more." "McDonald's favorite role"—and this conceals the contradictory tendencies—is as "host." One of the first variants of a mission statement from a major publisher called for various basic principles such as a "decentralized organization," "pluralism in program work," "employee relatedness," "social engagement," and "cultural orientation" were supposed to "stand in harmonious relationships" and not be allowed to "contradict one another."

Mission statements pass on value contradictions to an organization's employees, with this inconsistency only concealed with effort. On one hand, employees are meant to compete with one another as "entrepreneurs within the enterprise," yet they are also supposed to all pull together. Employees are expected to go their own way, yet they aren't supposed to lose sight of the company's overall goals. There should be enough space for unconventional thinkers to express their creativity and flexibility, but the company's resources should also be applied in the most effective manner possible.

In our experience, these sorts of "We'll make everybody happy at the same time and to the same extent" ideas rob corporate philosophies of their ability to provide orientation. Employees are constantly asked to choose between different contradictory values—they have to consider whether they push for a new, profitable coal-fired power plant, knowing that this decision would meet with disapproval from the majority of the population for environmental reasons. Managers have to decide whether, despite acceptable profits, they should let their employees go so that shareholders can get an even higher dividend. If mission statements try to cover up these everyday contradictions with formulations that are all too harmonious, this can result both in a loss of their impact and even have counterproductive consequences. Employees ask themselves how management can say such "pretty things" to them that are obviously so far removed from their everyday working world.

One of the variants that we most often propose is to go on the offensive and identify these opposing demands in mission statements as contradictions. We point out that "serving the customer," "obligations to shareholders," "fair treatment of suppliers," and "social responsibility" can come into conflict and that the organization has to decide on a case-by-case basis which demand will be assigned priority.

In a mission statement development process for a hotel chain, for example, consultants were pressing for the identification of the contradictory goals in the preamble to the corporate philosophy: the focus on a uniform corporate design *and* regional flair for each individual hotel, the priority for the success of each individual hotel *and* the chain's overall success. The personnel should meet specific quality standards *and* preserve naturalness and individuality in their appearance. The phrase "the right mixture of contradictory goals" emphasized that employees were expected to move independently within the space of these contradictory requirements.

The readiness to go with these kinds of "oppositional variants" exists in particular in organizations from the field of health care and social aid. In welfare organizations, this balancing act is pointed out directly in the mission statement; people with mental disabilities can participate in as many decision-making processes as possible, yet there are simultaneously attempts to uphold the legal standards of quality in organizations. In the mission statement of university hospitals, there is a reference to the fact that work there moves within a field of various expectations: expectations of patients, of society, the expectation that the precepts of economic efficiency will be upheld, and interests in research and teaching.

Admittedly, neither mission statements of the contradictory variety, nor those of the harmonization variety, provide specific structure for how employees act. The harmonization version blows smoke in employee's faces with its illusory notion of organizations, but the other version prepares them for organizational reality.

EXAMPLE

The Mission Statement of an Asian Development Bank— Positioning within Conflicting Priorities

In a mission statement project at a development bank, early discussions with management identified six fields of tension in the organization since its founding seven years earlier, and these fields would continue to generate tension in the coming years. These were the same conflicts faced by other development banks, both in developing and industrial countries.

- Orientation towards high profitability in their own banking business versus concentration on transactions that may be desirable in the context of development policy, yet present a significant economic risk.
- Focus on the main state client—the country's Ministry of Planning—or concentration on multiple state and parastatal clients.
- Homogeneous presentation of all regional departments (themes, loan volumes, strategic directions) versus allowing heterogeneity among departments that results from different regional circumstances in a country that consists of several islands.

- Emphasis of own profile as a national development bank versus emphasis on multinational cooperation projects, especially with the Asian Development Bank, which often offer better leverage yet often reduces the visibility of the bank's contribution.
- Focus on core competences—two segments in which the bank in Asia has developed a strong reputation—versus a broad focus on all loan projects that are currently desirable in terms of policy and are to a degree economically interesting.

In one of the first workshops with management, these fields of tension were discussed and more narrowly defined on the basis of proposals. Then employees were asked in one-hour workshops about their perceptions of the national development bank. Workshops and one-on-one discussions then focused in on how the development bank should situate itself strategically in the future. These assessments were captured quantitatively using a "++ | + | 0 | + | ++" scale (with the aid of points that the participants taped to the scale at the same time), and then participants provided reasons for their assessments. The results of the current and target assessments were then evaluated with quantitative (simply adding the scores up) and qualitative (compiling the key messages) means, and the results were presented to management in phase three. Most of the time in the workshop was spent trying to showcase the desired position in the fields of tension. During this process, there were expressions of a desire to more strongly emphasize some of these positions in the future (e.g., greater homogene-

> ity in presentation) as well as statements by management that the bank constantly has to make new decisions in this field of tension in its everyday work and that part of the employees' professionalism hinges on being able to make appropriate decisions in certain situations.

The more the mission statement development process went in the direction of internal or external publication, the stronger the pressure for "harmonization versions." Ultimately, not many companies will be in a position to apply the "contradictory version" in their official internal and external presentation, but the longer the contradictory requirements can be upheld in the process of mission statement creation, the closer to reality the conflicts will be that arise in such a process. The job for the people in charge of creating a mission statement is to keep talking about the contradictory requirements placed on the organization as long as possible, and to resist the urge to defuse all of these contradictions into harmonizing formulas.

3.2 Between Orientation towards Overarching Modes and the Specifics of an Organization

Mission statements are often drawn on generally accepted values, and because almost all organizations are oriented towards these generally accepted values, their philosophies are therefore similar. Almost every corporate philosophy mentions a "focus on the customer," praise for employees as "the most important resource," and celebration of "social responsibility." With regard to internal coordination mechanisms, almost every corporate philosophy calls for "employees to be entrepreneurs within the enterprise" and that they should treat other departments as "internal customers."

Aspects from current management models are frequently integrated into mission statements. Long ago, many companies had principles that spoke of factories as "clockworks" or of "factories without people"; today, the dominant keywords tend to be "total quality management," "customer focus," or "boundary less organization." In the 1990s, many mission statements contained commitments to "Lean Management" and "Business Process Reengineering" which were then replaced, once the trend was over, by self-descriptions such as "learning organizations" or "knowledge-based companies."

The approach to mission statements at "pioneering organizations" and the assumption of social values that are generally seen as "good practice" is called "organizational mimetics." Companies, administrations, hospitals, schools and universities all strive to commit themselves to generally accepted social values such as environmental protection, democracy and sustainability, or to orient themselves towards the core ideas of pioneering companies that industry currently views as the "best practice."

The incorporation of these principles into their own mission statements, the integration of current popular management concepts, or the hiring of fashionable consultants or managers—all of this has the function of producing legitimacy. In the 1970s, John W. Meyer and Brian Rowan had already demonstrated that companies, in order to be successful, do not just have to organize themselves so efficiently that they can refinance themselves and kick out profits that are tolerable for shareholders; they can also find acceptance in their environment—in policies, mass media, and sometimes also in science. Social acceptance is ever more important for administrations, hospitals, universities and businesses that have a development mandate that goes beyond producing profits. Mission statements that connect to generally accepted values are an instrument used with ever greater frequency to attain this legitimacy. It certainly makes sense for manager to refer to generally accepted values that relieve them from the burden of explaining themselves and that are also recognized outside of the organization (Meyer and Rowan 1977).

But using generally accepted values conceals a major risk: the more organizations commit to the same values, and often with very similar verbiage, the more the specific character of individual organizations suffers (Deephouse 1999). When reading mission statements, people often have the impression that other organizations have overtaken the copy-and-paste button, or that consulting firms and advertising agencies have plagiarized text elements from other corporate philosophies. Smaller organizations or organizational units that are charged by their holding company or by legal regulations to come up with a mission statement often seem to resort to borrowing proven formulas from others.

The risks of very similar mission statements lie at two levels. The orientation effect for an individual employee is very low if the value at hand is not specific to the organization, but rather is a value observed by all organizations, and the mission statement loses legitimacy as similarity increases. A mission statement that does not attempt to say what is special or unique about an organization cannot produce any legitimacy.

We therefore recommend keeping to a bare minimum the proportion of general value statements that are found in all corporate philosophies. Many Western European or North American companies can do away with commitments to "following laws," "protecting the environment," "combating corruption," "focus on the customer," or waxing grandiloquent about "employees as the most important resource." This is different of course for companies in which such practices are not already common practice. For a German electronics corporation that has secured contracts in Latin America, Eastern Europe, Asia or Africa by paying bribes, it may very well be advisable—for reasons of legitimation to the outside world and orientation inside—to include a proactive, extensive statement on "preventing corruption." One North American fruit company developed a reputation for supporting dictatorships in Central America, perpetrating environmental destruction on large plantations, and being responsible for its employees' health problems. In such cases, it makes sense, both for the company's employees and for its external observers, for the mission statement to include commitments to democracy, the environment and occupational health.

We believe that, in parallel to the reduction or complete elimination of statements found in almost all mission statements, it is important to final formulations that highlight the particular qualities of the respective organization. To check whether the criterion of specificity has been met in the mission statement, we use various tools in our workshops.

THEORY

1. "What Is Memorable"

Especially in companies that already have a mission statement or have even had several, it is an interesting exercise to ask employees which aspects of the core principles they remember. Consultants can ask this question in workshops, or it can be used in discussions in preparation for a new mission statement process. It is often instructive whenever a top manager asks a few employees this question two or three years after creating a corporate philosophy. What is interesting is, in many cases, how little of the philosophy catches on. This happens because the old mission statements often contain too many self-evident facts. Example: This question proved particularly interesting at a major German auto manufacturer because several production employees could not remember a single aspect of their mission statement, despite the fact that they were actually required to carry an abridged version printed on a plastic card.

2. "The Surprise Survey"

In the phase in which management has developed the contours of the future mission statement and put it up for an initial discussion with employees, it is worth asking which elements of the mission statement surprise employees. You can also use this question to evaluate an existing mission statement. Example: At a French bank, almost all of the employees expressed surprise that the bank had committed in its mission statement to the idea that not every internal document had to have the perfection of a document that would be provided to the outside world.

3. "The Difference Review"

One way to assess quality in the late stage of corporate philosophy development is to compare the product with four or five mission statements from companies in the same industry. Key statements are taken from these mission statements—and from the one under development—and anonymized. If the employees cannot identify their own organization from the key statements, this is a clear indication that organizational mimetics have penetrated too deeply. Example: The similarity of mission statements in retail companies is particularly striking. If we look at the corporate philosophies of Home Depot and Lowe's, for example, it is quite a challenge to work out what is specific about them.

4. "That's Not What We Want to Be"

It is always easy for organizations to say how they would like to be perceived. It is difficult, however, to say what an attractive attribution would be from its own employees, customers or external observers. This means that organizations would rather avoid surprises in such perceptions so that they can position themselves clearly. To find this out in our workshops, we ask managers or employees a series of three questions: "What are we?" "What are we as well (or perhaps actually not)?" "What are we not?" The answers to the third question often provide clarity as to how the organization should be positioned in the eyes of others. Example: At a large luxury goods company that has successfully positioned itself over the last twenty years, we discovered that people "perceive the company as fashionable, but not as a trendsetter in fashion." We were able to show that although the company was focused on profits, they did not want to be a capitalist company driven by the capital markets.

5. "Bullshit Bingo"

The trend towards trendy vocabulary has led to a certain popularity of Bullshit Bingo in organizations. In Bullshit Bingo, we make up, before a meeting, workshop or conference, a list of frequently used but ultimately meaningless keywords, such as synergy, sustainability, vision, cooperative leadership style, globalization, learning organization, or teamwork. The Bingo players then watch the presentations and make a note of each time a presenter uses one of these terms. If a player gets a horizontal or vertical line of keywords, he calls out (hopefully softly) "Bingo!" and has won.

It's unclear how often Bullshit Bingo is actually played, or if it has only developed a reputation due to its distribution over email. There are now versions of Bullshit Bingo circulating on the Internet that are specific to organizational types, industries and companies. They give a good impression of which buzzwords employees find particularly meaningless. An especially tough test for a mission statement that is under development is to take a look at it and see how many terms from the Bullshit Bingo list show up. You can either use the generic versions of Bullshit Bingo, or the company-specific versions.

3.3 Between Ideals and Describing the World

Mission statements and corporate philosophies often read like the stringing together of ideals about how a company, administration or hospital ought to be. The mission statement of Volkswagen, for example, put forward the idea that the company should optimize the goals of "sustainability, environmental sustainability, social responsibility, increasing value, transparency, and control." Novartis says that its goal is to "positively influence people's lives, satisfy needs, and to exceed expectations."

There are good reasons for the tendency to compile visions and ideas of the future. The world of possible futures always seems more attractive than the often difficult realities of everyday life in which a company, administration or non-profit organization exists. But this is precisely the problem. When the future receives too much emphasis, the mission statement begins to present what "organizations are not." Mission statements frequently turn out to be flat because there is always the danger that the "image of the future" will contrast too strongly with reality.

It therefore makes sense to be very careful when setting up the elements that point to the future—the vision aspects—and not to make them too flowery. Statements such as, "We want to be the most innovative company in our industry" fizzle out because the term "innovative" allows for too many interpretations. A better statement would be, "In each of the pharmaceutical markets we serve, we strive to offer at least one medication that belongs to the top three sellers in the market."

Instead of overloading a mission statement with futures, visions and ideals, we recommend using it to offer employees, clients, customers and partners a precise description of the setting in which an organization moves and how the organization wants to see itself triangulated within this setting. For the national Asian development bank, for example, a mission statement project used the following questions to define the relevant environmental conditions: What is the relationship to the state client, and what role do new possible state, parastatal or private customers play for the organization? How is the bank's self-understanding as a development bank understood, and what role do cooperative agreements with a number of multinational development banks play? Does the bank want to generate major effects with the highest possible loans, or does it want to use smaller projects to make its mark in a difficult environment? How much homogeneity does the bank want in its external appearance, and how much heterogeneity is it prepared to allow? In what way should departments compete internally from resources, and what role does internal cooperation play in this? The value of a mission statement does not consist so much in its ambitious visions, but rather in the precise description of the environment in which the organization is located.

In exploratory phases in particular, it makes sense to reach an agreement about the organization's environment and its current position in it. But the formulation process has also shown that recipients of mission statements receive orientation when there is a precise description of where exactly the organization is located, and in which environment.

3.4 The Same Mission Statement for Everyone, or Different Versions

The fact that the same mission statement—directed at customers, suppliers, partner organizations, politicians, the mass media, and potential new employees—also reaches the organization's own staff leads to a problem in many organizations. Staff have only have a limited interest in an attractive front because their everyday work grants them views and glimpses of the organization's backstage life. From this perspective, mission statements often have an off-putting effect on an organization's own employees because it presents to them an airbrushed front that is meant for external audiences and has little to do with the backstage that they know to be closer to reality.

Our recommendation for action is therefore to decouple the mission statement meant for external consumption—at least partially—from the mission statement discussed with employees. Admittedly, such an explicitly expressed thought may be quite unusual for some managers. Normally it is considered good style when people act in companies as though the messages transmitted to the outside world are identical to those lived and preached inside the company. Such efforts are carried out under the banner of authenticity, suggesting that there be as few as discrepancies as possible between the front and back offices at an organization. Reality looks quite different, and for good reasons.

It is clear to every worker in a company that communication has to be adjusted to respective discussion partners. One department's half-baked idea should not always be discussed immediately with other departments. All internal deliberations should not be shared with suppliers, despite all of the postulates of transparency. Not all quality problems should be relayed immediately to a customer. Information for shareholders should not assume the same form as information for employees.

If a company, administration or hospital gives everyone the same information, there are only two possibilities: the information must be so abstract that it is equally well received by all audiences—with the danger of it being watered down, and that employees, expecting clear directions and orientation, react with cynicism. Or there is only one single form of communication that is applied to all of the different target groups and is perhaps suitable for one and highly problematic for another.

We can see this in the example of an automotive company that uses nearly the same communication strategy for its employees as it does for its customers. In a video made for its employees, with the motto, "It is you," there are repeated references to individual employees. We suppose that communication strategies that use the same formats and content for employees as for customers tend to have a rather counterproductive effect.

But how can we develop a mission statement that is custom-tailored for audiences without making the discrepancy all too clear?

Some companies do a point-by-point breakdown by developing mission statements for specific target groups. There is a mission statement oriented towards shareholders, one that defines supplier relationships, a mission statement for customers, and a mission statement for employees. The advantage of this approach is that the organization's appearance, and the kinds of visions it cultivates, can be presented in a way that is very audience-specific. But this approach also has disadvantages, in addition to the effort of coordination: By creating multiple mission statements, it is not clear how the organization intends to proceed if the demands from shareholders, suppliers, customers and employees come into conflict. The coherence between the mission statements tailored to specific audiences must nevertheless be assured, because all of the target groups usually also have access to the mission statements of the other groups.

A second variant is to formulate the various mission statements in different and specific ways. You could create for example a comprehensive mission statement that could provide the basis for encounters between managers and employees. This mission statement is condensed in a second step in such a way that the result is a credo partially scrubbed of its sharp edges and specifications that can also be presented to customers, suppliers and shareholders.

A third version resembles the previous one, but follows the approach even more closely. It makes sense to articulate explicit, surprising statements when crafting a mission statement. At this point it is important to turn off the alarm bells in your head that automatically ring whenever you start thinking that the mission statement is going to end up published on your website. The phase in which understanding emerges between managers and employees is a particularly auspicious moment for the management-led mission statement to offer orientation. Whenever the communication of a mission statement to the outside world is at issue, people retain a few explicit and surprising statements but pack them into a presentation form that is appropriate for dealing with customers.

EXAMPLE

The Example of a U.S. Publisher— The Near-Secret Drafting of a Mission Statement

A large U.S. publisher makes 95% of its revenues from a large state client. The publisher prints documents with high security requirements; they have to be high-quality prints and sometimes have to be produced at short notice. The publisher is cautiously starting to open up to other state, parastatal and private customers so that it can reduce its reliance on its one client. These first cautious steps lead to the main client doubting whether it will continue to be treated in such a privileged way by the publisher and whether the security standards can be upheld. At the same time, there is uncertainty among the employees about how they should communicate with the main client. Should they think of themselves as the "extended arm" of the client? Only describe the client as a "privileged customer"? Or merely as one client among others?

The management makes decisions in a mission statement process to provide "more clarity" for employees while simultaneously articulating a position to the customer. The challenge here is that what the publisher has told its employees—that they want to slowly open up to new customers—cannot be communicated to the outside world because it would impact the relationship to their main client. The publisher was spun off a few years ago from their current main client. Due to the joint history between the two firms, the companies have a very close relationship, so there is a risk that internal documents, PowerPoint presentations to the board, or an inwardly directed mission statement could show up in the main client's hands.

How can the publisher offer a new direction to employees without unsettling the client? The management decides to only use handwritten flipcharts and boards in the second phase of mission statement development, the concept development phase. This reduces the likelihood that information can be passed on to the main client (it would not be possible to simply copy documents). What is more important, however, is that the new direction is presented in a form that enables a signal to the main client, if necessary, that these are only initial considerations and that nothing is chiseled in stone.

This approach allows the management to cut the Gordian knot. On one side is the politically smooth mission statement that can be presented without hesitation to shareholders, customers and suppliers; on the other hand, the intense discussion with employees, documented by handwritten statements on flipcharts and boards, helped point employees in a new direction.

3.5 Mission Statements between Central Initiation and Decentral Anchoring

The initiative for developing mission statements almost always comes from the top of an organization. The organization's standing is not necessarily irrelevant to the normal employee on the assembly line or the orderly in the cancer ward, but the head of the organization is ultimately responsible for its reputation. This also explains why the top management, and in the best-case scenario those tasked with developing the mission statement, hang on to the canon of values with special dedication. If a decision for or against a mission statement process has to be made, top management is typically ready to assign funds to the project, while middle-management employees, who are strongly integrated in the operational side of the business, frequently express doubts.

This special initiative by the top management is associated with its top position in the organization. While the heads of such departments as product development, research and development, production or sales feel primarily responsible for optimizing their respective fields, top management's job is to integrate various work processes, to negotiate conflicts between different fields, and to present the organization as a unified whole, both inwardly and outwardly. In mission statement processes, we see engagement from the top management and reservation from middle management; this results almost automatically from the hierarchical division of labor within an organization.

This is why it is typical to describe mission statement processes as a management issue that is largely executed top-down. When a company repositions itself, this is why the mission statement is frequently devised at the top of the organization and then announced to the employees. During a merger, the new organizational leadership often pulls an (almost) ready mission statement out of their pocket, assuming that it will facilitate integration in the organization.

While it may very well be functional a lot of the time to develop strategies in a small circle of people and then apply them to an organization, a mission statement that is imposed top-down is counterproductive. At the end, only the boss and the staff members who have been assigned the job of creating and communicating the canon of values know the mission statement. After (!) the creation of the mission statement, this often leads to helpless measures: Employees are informed about the mission statement with expensive advertising campaigns, summoned to seminars where they are to be inculcated with the principles of the corporate philosophy, or the staff are even forced to carry around summaries of the mission statement on plastic cards.

The bottom-to-top development of a mission statement represents the other extreme. In the 1980s, when the first experiments with the development of mission statements were conducted, there were companies that used surveys (sometimes standardized, sometimes not) to gather the opinions of every (!) employee as to what they believe the organization's visions, values and guidelines should be. Relevant statements were distilled from the results, sometimes with the aid of complicated calculation methods, and prepared into a mission statement for the organization.

This approach had the advantage of involving employees very early on in the development of the canon of values, thereby broadening the process at a very early stage. But this approach also has two problems: the first one is the fact that this bottom-to-top process sends the message that employees make decisions about significant aspects of the organization—a message that poses a discrepancy to the everyday experiences of employees in most companies, administrations and hospitals. And this bottom-to-top procedure often leads to the selection of the lowest common denominator, yielding a mission statement without contours.

This is why most mission statement processes have developed a common practice of coupling both bottom-to-top and top-down development processes. When we put it in such a simple way, however, this principle remains a platitude that everyone can agree with at first. The challenges are in the details: how exactly can we connect the initiatives coming from headquarters with the involvement of employees? In what form should decision-making and discussion processes be organized? Which aspects should be communicated top-down? And which from bottom to top? At which moments should few organizational members be involved? And at which moment should the maximum number of members participate? And in what form should many people participate?

There is a proven five-step approach that alternates between moments when few people are involved and moments when many people are involved. We can distinguish roughly between an experimental phase that determines which perceptions are dominant in the organization and which frames of reference management wants, and another phase in which management develops and discusses specific contexts. Different guiding questions define the process in each step.

In the first phase, a workshop with management, lasting no more than one day and with no more than eight to ten people clarifies the question of whether the organization or the organizational unit wants to go through a mission statement process. Because middle management, shaped as it is by the operational business, often expresses doubts about the meaningfulness of such mission statements, it makes sense to call for a discussion about a decision to go through a corporate philosophy process. This phase also frequently includes finding agreement about what the process should be called. Because the term "mission statement" has already been used by previous processes, it is appropriate sometimes to choose other names such as "self-understanding," "compass" or "mission."

While very few people are involved in the first phase, the second phase calls in several employees from the organization. In the discussions with employees, people use very short, often only one-hour mini-workshops with ten to fifteen employees. In these mini-workshops, they are only asked about their opinion on the current situation in the organization in relation to previously defined central themes. Employees should not be asked about how they want to position the organization; this signals that such decisions are the prerogative of management. Selected employees can be called together to these mini-workshops, which have a uniform script; it's also easy to integrate them into regular appointments, such as departmental meetings, or cross-functional meetings. The survey about the status quo is then done in individual meetings, or sometimes in small workshops with upper management; requests for positioning are also surveyed. Quantitative surveys can also be integrated into the status quo query, which for example can find out where employees believe the organization is located in strategic terms—not because the resulting figures lead to specific actions, but in order to attract attention in the following phase by means of a quantitative evaluation (often very primitive).

Only a few people, typically from the organization's upper management, are involved in the third phase. We play back the results from the experiment in a workshop that usually only takes half a day. What is interesting at this point of the process is the assessment of the current situation and the ideas about target positioning from the upper management. This discussion provides material that is developed into key statements for positioning; these are then presented in a more refined form one more time after the workshop, and then sent off for a decision from management. In many companies, this is where the development process for mission statements ends, and the key statements are shared with employees in a brochure. We find the following concept development phase, however, to be central.

In the fourth phase, the process widens out once again. The preliminary (!) key statements developed by management are then offered up for discussion again among the employees. These statements are formulated on one or two flipcharts or boards and discussed with a representative from upper management in one-hour mini-workshops with ten to fifteen participants. These mini-workshops can either be convened as extra appointments, integrated into regular employee schedules, or conducted at an interaction marketplace after lunch. It is preferable for the upper management representatives not just to introduce the key statements in their own departments, but also to a mixed internal audience. Often it is sufficient if each upper management representative conducts four to five of these mini-workshops. The main function of these mini-workshops is to generate a discussion between upper management and employees about the current and target situation in the organization, while at the same time performing a reality check on the key statements formulated by management.

In the fifth phase, there is a final vote on the guiding principle statements, typically in a half-day workshop, but sometimes in a normal meeting of the top management. Depending on how precise these statements are meant to be, there can still be controversies at this point, and they should be promoted intentionally because such debates can result in very interesting perspectives on the work that comes later.

4. The Relevance of the Mission Statement Process and Cultivating the Final Product—Conclusion

In many cases, the finished mission statement shows up in a high-gloss brochure. In some companies, it is chiseled in stone over the gates, like the Ten Commandments, to present the corporate philosophy as something close to sacred. In other companies, the mission statement is one of the first features that opens up when you visit their homepage.

There are good reasons why mission statements are presented in glossy brochures, engraved into stone, or given prominence as pop-ups on a website: they suggest permanence and durability. This signals that the statement is not a "vision of the week," "a value of the month," or a "mission statement of the annual lottery"; it is a statement to which the organization has committed itself over the long term. As we have shown, every organization—every company, every administration, every hospital and definitely every lobby organization, every political party and every non-governmental organization—depends on the construction of an attractive front to external parties—customers, suppliers, partner organizations, politicians, the mass media, and potential new employees. The shinier and stable a mission statement seems, the better suited it is for the decoration of the organization's display side.

Frequently, however, it is precisely the principles that are hewn in stone, printed on posters and in high-gloss brochures that create problems with consistency. Not a few companies have mission statements printed on posters that present a direction that is no longer *en vogue*. These "obsolete" or "worn-out" mission statements simply stay on the walls because nobody feels responsible for replacing them with new ones.

This is why it makes more sense to concentrate more on the process of creating a mission statement, and less on the finished product. Agreements between the management and employees about a canon of values are reached during the process of generating a mission statement, not in the moment of its presentation. It is the difficult process of developing a mission statement in which principles are not just defined and specified, but also distributed within the organization. In the hackneyed words of the esoteric scene, when it comes to creating mission statements, the journey is the destination.

A rule of thumb in traditional mission statement processes is the 80-20 rule. In a classical mission statement process, 20% of the budget, the manpower management has reserved for the project, the staff positions and external service providers are applied to the phase of experimentation and the creation of the mission statement. The remaining 80% of the budget is expended after the corporate philosophy is on its feet—for the precise wording, the design of the image brochure, printing, announcement events and the organization of follow-up events in which, for example, management discusses in midday meetings how to comply with these core principles. In the approach we have introduced here, the real effects take hold in the experimentation phase, the development of the mission statement and the discussion of the initial drafts. Accordingly, 80% of the budget is invested in the time of managers, staff positions and external service providers who are working on this phase. A maximum of 20% of management's time, budget and expenses for external service providers are then—if at all—required after the completion of the corporate philosophy.

In order for the 80-20 principle to work, management has to present a very thoroughly developed mission statement for discussion after the 80% phase. Of course, you can produce a "complete corporate philosophy" and then have the managers run a broad rollout to announce it to the employees. But this robs you of the opportunity to discuss the canon of values with employees; after all, this is only about information, and critical objections or meaningful proposals remain inconsequential. To bring this point home one more time: if it is still necessary, after (!) the creation of a mission statement, to go through an elaborate process to announce the corporate philosophy to employees, then something went wrong during the development of the canon of values.

Bibliography

Bart, Christopher K. 1997. "Sex, Lies, and Mission Statements: Why Aren't Mission Statements Getting the Credit They Deserve, or the Results Managers and Experts Have Expected?" *Business Horizons* 40 (6): 9–18.

Blair-Loy, Mary, Amy S. Wharton, and Jerry Goodstein. 2011. "Exploring the Relationship Between Mission Statements and Work-Life Practices in Organizations." *Organization Studies* 32: 427–50.

Brunsson, Nils. 1989. *The Organization of Hypocrisy: Talk, Decisions and Actions in Organizations.* Chichester et al. John Wiley & Sons.

Collins, Jim, and Jerry I. Porras. 2005. *Immer erfolgreich: Die Strategien der Top Unternehmen.* München: dtv.

Davidson, Hugh. 2002. *The Committed Enterprise.* London/New York: Routledge.

Deephouse, David L. 1999. "To Be Different or to Be the Same? It's a Question (and Theory) of Strategic Balance." *Strategic Management Journal* 20: 147–66.

Kaplan, Robert S., and David P. Norton. 1996. *The Balanced Scorecard: Translating Strategy into Action.* Boston: Harvard Business School Press.

Kaplan, Robert S., and David P. Norton. 2008. *Execution Premium: Linking Strategy to Operations for Competitive Advantage.* Boston: Harvard Business School Press.

Kay, Ira T., and Bruce N. Pfau. 2001. *The Human Capital Edge*. New York: McGraw-Hill.

Kühl, Stefan. 2011. *Organisationen: Eine sehr kurze Einführung*. Wiesbaden: VS Verlag für Sozialwissenschaften.

Lewin, Kurt. 1951. "Problems of Research in Social Psychology." In *Field Theory in Social Science: Selected Theoretical Papers by Kurt Lewin*, edited by Dorwin Cartwright, 155–69. New York: Harper & Row.

Luhmann, Niklas. 1964. *Funktionen und Folgen formaler Organisation*. Berlin: Duncker & Humblot.

Luhmann, Niklas. 1972. *Rechtssoziologie*. Reinbek: Rowohlt.

Luhmann, Niklas. 1977. "Probleme eines Parteiprogramms." In *Freiheit und Sachzwang: Beiträge zu Ehren Helmut Schelskys*, edited by Horst Baier, 167–81. Opladen: WDV.

Luhmann, Niklas. 2000. *Organisation und Entscheidung*. Opladen: WDV.

March, James G., and Herbert A. Simon. 1958. *Organizations*. New York: John Wiley & Sons.

Meyer, John W., and Brian Rowan. 1977. "Institutionalized Organizations. Formal Structure as Myth and Ceremony." *American Journal of Sociology* 83: 340–63.

Rigby, Darrell. 2003. *Management Tools*. Boston: Bain and Company.

Rottenburg, Richard. 1996. "When Organization Travels: on Intercultural Translation." In *Translating Organizational Change*, edited by Czarniawska, Barbara, and Guje Sevón, 191–240. Berlin/New York: Walter de Gruyter.

Weick, Karl E. 1976. "Educational Organizations as Loosely Coupled Systems." *Administrative Science Quarterly* 21: 1–19.

Whitley, Richard. 1984. "The Fragmented State of Management Studies: Reasons and Consequences." *Journal of Management Studies* 21 (3): 331–48.

www.ingramcontent.com/pod-product-compliance
Lightning Source LLC
Chambersburg PA
CBHW020303030426
42336CB00010B/880